How to Develop Student Creativity

Robert J. Sternberg
is IBM Professor of
Psychology and Education
at Yale University. He is
coauthor of *Defying the
Crowd: Cultivating
Creativity in a Culture of
Conformity* and editor of
The Nature of Creativity.
Sternberg can be reached at
the Department of
Psychology, Yale University,
Box 208205, New Haven,
CT 06520-8205.
Phone: (203) 432-4633.
Fax: (203) 432-8317.

Wendy M. Williams
is research scientist in the
Department of Psychology
at Yale University. She is
author of *The Reluctant
Reader.* Williams can be
reached at the Department
of Psychology, Yale
University, Box 208205,
New Haven, CT 06520-8205.

Personally, I would sooner have written *Alice in Wonderland* than the whole *Encyclopedia Britannica*.

—*Stephen Leacock*

The creation of a thousand forests is in one acorn.

—*Ralph Waldo Emerson*

What another would have done as well as you, do not do it. What another would have said as well as you, do not say it. What another would have written as well, do not write it. Be faithful to that which exists nowhere but in yourself—and thus make yourself indispensable.

—*Andre Gide*

Too many people think they are being creative when they are just being different.

—*anonymous*

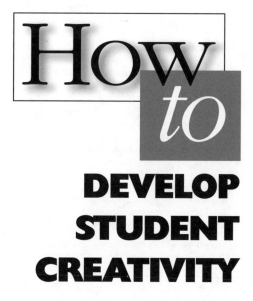

How *to*

DEVELOP
STUDENT
CREATIVITY

Robert J. Sternberg and Wendy M. Williams

Association for Supervision and Curriculum Development
Alexandria, Virginia

Association for Supervision and Curriculum Development
1250 N. Pitt Street • Alexandria, Virginia 22314
Telephone: (703) 549-9110 • Fax: (703) 299-8631

Gene R. Carter, *Executive Director*
Michelle Terry, *Assistant Executive Director, Program Development*
Ronald S. Brandt, *Assistant Executive Director*
Nancy Modrak, *Managing Editor, ASCD Books*
Darcie Simpson, *Associate Editor*
Gary Bloom, *Manager, Design and Production Services*
Karen Monaco, *Senior Designer*
Tracey A. Smith, *Print Production Coordinator*
Dina Murray, *Production Assistant*
Valerie Sprague, *Desktop Publisher*

Development of this book was supported by a grant from the James S. McDonnell
Foundation and by a government grant under the Javits Act Program (Grant
#R206R50001) as administered by the Office of Educational Research and
Improvement, U.S. Department of Education. Grantees undertaking such projects are
encouraged to freely express their professional judgment. This book, therefore, does
not necessarily represent positions or policies of the U.S. government and no official
endorsement should be inferred.

ASCD publications present a variety of viewpoints. The views expressed or implied
in this book should not be interpreted as official positions of the Association.

Printed in the United States of America.

ASCD Stock No. 196073
p8/96
ASCD Members $8.95
Nonmembers $10.95

Library of Congress Cataloging-in-Publication Data
Sternberg, Robert J.
    How to develop student creativity / Robert J. Sternberg and Wendy M. Williams.
        p.   cm.
    Includes bibliographical references.
    ISBN 0-87120-265-4 (pbk.)
    1. Creative thinking—Study and teaching. I. Williams, Wendy M., (Wendy
Melissa), 1960- . II. Association for Supervision and Curriculum Development.
III. Title.
    LB1590.5.S84 1996
    370.15'7—dc20   96-10094
                                                                 CIP

00 99 98 97 96   5 4 3 2 1

Introduction:
Theory of Creativity

"Alice is brilliant, but she doesn't have a drop of creative talent."

"Barbara is wonderfully creative, but she does poorly on standardized tests."

"Carlos always has interesting approaches to problems, but he just doesn't fit into the traditional school environment."

How many times have we, as teachers, administrators, researchers, or parents, heard remarks like these? And how many times have we concluded that abilities are etched in stone, inexplicable, and unchangeable? You can learn and teach creative thinking by using the 25 strategies that we describe in this book. Use these strategies to develop creativity in yourself, in your students, and in your colleagues and staff members. Our strategies are based on the investment theory, a psychological theory of creativity, but any one strategy is consistent with many other theories. Read about other views of creativity to see how different views lead to similar recommendations for developing creativity (Amabile 1983, Boden 1992, Gardner 1993, Ghiselin 1985, Gruber 1981, John-Steiner 1987, Rubenson and Runco 1992, Simonton 1988, Sternberg 1988a).

Buying Low and Selling High

The investment theory of creativity (Sternberg and Lubart 1995) asserts that creative thinkers are like good investors: They buy low and sell high. Whereas investors do so in the world of finance, creative people do so in the world of ideas. Creative people generate ideas that are like undervalued stocks (stocks with a low price-to-earning ratio), and both are generally rejected by the public. When creative ideas are proposed, they are often viewed as bizarre, useless, and even foolish, and are summarily rejected, and the person proposing them regarded with suspicion and perhaps even disdain and derision.

Creative ideas are both novel and valuable. Why, then, are they rejected? Because the creative innovator stands up to vested interests and defies the crowd and its interests. The crowd does not maliciously or willfully reject creative notions; rather it does not realize, and often does not want to realize, that the proposed idea represents a valid and superior way of thinking. The crowd generally perceives opposition to the status quo as annoying, offensive, and reason enough to ignore innovative ideas.

Evidence abounds that creative ideas are rejected (Sternberg and Lubart 1995). Initial reviews of major works of literature and art are often negative. Toni Morrison's *Tar Baby* received negative reviews when it was first published, as did Sylvia Plath's *The Bell Jar.* The first exhibition in Munich of the Norwegian painter, Edvard Munch, opened and closed the same day because of the strong negative response from the critics. Some of the greatest scientific papers are rejected by not one but several journals before being published. John Garcia, a distinguished biopsychologist, was summarily denounced when he first proposed that classical conditioning could be produced in a single trial of learning (Garcia and Koelling 1966).

From the investment view, then, the creative person buys low by presenting a unique idea and attempts to convince other people of its value. After convincing others that the idea is worthy, which increases the perceived value of the investment, the creative person sells high by leaving the idea to others and moving to another idea. Although people typically want others to love their ideas, immediate universal applause for an idea usually indicates that it is not particularly creative.

Foster creativity by buying low and selling high in the world of ideas—defy the crowd. Creativity is as much an attitude toward life as a matter of ability. We routinely witness creativity in young children, but it is hard to find in older children and adults because their creative potential has been suppressed by a society that encourages intellectual conformity. We begin to suppress children's natural creativity when we expect them to color within the lines in their coloring books.

Balancing Analytic, Synthetic, and Practical Abilities

Creative work requires applying and balancing three abilities that can all be developed (Sternberg 1985, 1988b; Sternberg and Lubart 1995).

• **Synthetic ability** is what we typically think of as creativity. It is the ability to generate novel and interesting ideas. Often the person we call creative is a particularly good synthetic thinker who makes connections between things that other people don't recognize spontaneously.

• **Analytic ability** is typically considered to be critical thinking ability. A person with this skill analyzes and evaluates ideas. Everyone, even the most creative person you know, has better and worse ideas. Without well-developed analytic ability, the creative thinker is as likely to pursue bad ideas as to pursue good ones. The creative individual uses analytic ability to work out the implications of a creative idea and to test it.

• **Practical ability** is the ability to translate theory into practice and abstract ideas into practical accomplishments. An implication of the investment theory of creativity is that good ideas do not sell themselves. The creative person uses practical ability to convince other people that an idea is worthy. For example, every organization has a set of ideas that dictate how things, or at least some things, should be done. To propose a new procedure you must sell it by convincing others that it is better than the old one. Practical ability is also used to recognize ideas that have a potential audience.

༄ ༄ ༄

Creativity requires a balance among synthetic, analytic, and practical abilities. The person who is only synthetic may come up with innovative ideas, but cannot recognize or sell them. The person who is only analytic may be an excellent critic of other people's ideas, but is not likely to generate creative ideas. The person who is only practical may be an excellent salesperson, but is as likely to sell ideas or products of little or no value as to sell genuinely creative ideas.

Encourage and develop creativity by teaching students to find a balance among synthetic, analytic, and practical thinking. A creative attitude is at least as important as creative-thinking skills (Schank 1988)—just ask a teacher for a self-description. I've never heard a teacher self-described as a suppressor of creativity. The majority of teachers want to encourage creativity in their students, but they are not sure how to do so. Those teachers and you can use the 25 strategies presented in this book to develop creativity in yourselves, your students, and others around you.

Using just a few of our 25 strategies based on the investment theory of creativity (Sternberg and Lubart 1995) can produce results in yourself as well as in others. Although we present the strategies in terms of teachers and students, they apply equally to administrators working with teachers, parents working with children, or people trying to develop their own creativity. The strategies are easy to use and are outlined in Figure 1.

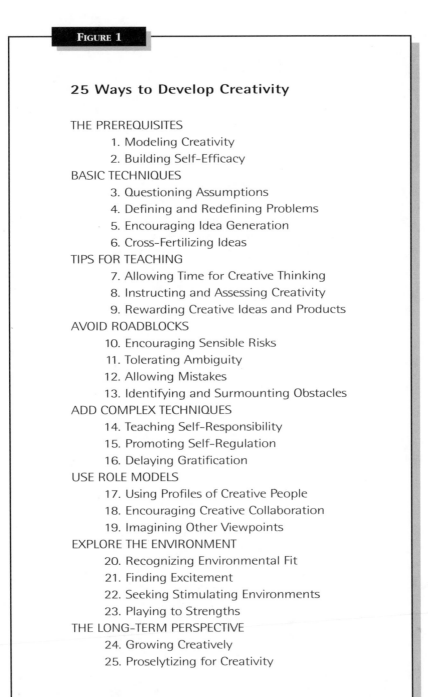

FIGURE 1

25 Ways to Develop Creativity

THE PREREQUISITES
    1. Modeling Creativity
    2. Building Self-Efficacy
BASIC TECHNIQUES
    3. Questioning Assumptions
    4. Defining and Redefining Problems
    5. Encouraging Idea Generation
    6. Cross-Fertilizing Ideas
TIPS FOR TEACHING
    7. Allowing Time for Creative Thinking
    8. Instructing and Assessing Creativity
    9. Rewarding Creative Ideas and Products
AVOID ROADBLOCKS
    10. Encouraging Sensible Risks
    11. Tolerating Ambiguity
    12. Allowing Mistakes
    13. Identifying and Surmounting Obstacles
ADD COMPLEX TECHNIQUES
    14. Teaching Self-Responsibility
    15. Promoting Self-Regulation
    16. Delaying Gratification
USE ROLE MODELS
    17. Using Profiles of Creative People
    18. Encouraging Creative Collaboration
    19. Imagining Other Viewpoints
EXPLORE THE ENVIRONMENT
    20. Recognizing Environmental Fit
    21. Finding Excitement
    22. Seeking Stimulating Environments
    23. Playing to Strengths
THE LONG-TERM PERSPECTIVE
    24. Growing Creatively
    25. Proselytizing for Creativity

1 The Prerequisites

Modeling Creativity

The most powerful way to develop creativity in your students is to be a role model. Children develop creativity not when you tell them to, but when you show them.

The teachers you most remember from your school days are not those who crammed the most content into their lectures. The teachers you remember are those whose thoughts and actions served as your role model. Most likely they balanced teaching content with teaching you how to think with and about that content.

Williams' most memorable teacher was a college professor of modern American poetry. His message was that each of his students had the talent to write poetry and that each of us would be writing it by the end of the term. His enthusiasm was contagious, and his teaching was spiced with advice on how to start a poem or an essay ("spill the beans!") and how to write succinctly ("write the way you talk—but without the repetition!"). He encouraged us to write poems in the forms of the great poets and then to develop our own styles. He read our poems aloud to the class (without identifying the author) and criticized and praised our work.

By the end of the term we were all writing poetry, much of it quite good, almost all of it better than we had thought possible. The professor was a role model for supporting creative performance—he was not judgmental, he encouraged new ideas, he praised what worked, he explained what didn't work, and he believed in every student. He used specific techniques to encourage us, but Williams remembers his enthusiasm and personal example.

$$\text{ॐ} \quad \text{ॐ} \quad \text{ॐ}$$

Occasionally, we'll teach a workshop on developing creativity and someone inevitably asks exactly how to develop creativity. Bad start. We can get you started, but we can't tell you precisely what to do or how to do it. You cannot follow a recipe for developing creativity—first, because there is none; second, because such a recipe would provide *uncreative* role-modeling. Instead, follow the guidelines in this book and show students your creative process to encourage them in their own creative thinking.

Serving as a role model for creative behavior is essential if you expect students and colleagues to engage in creative behavior. So think carefully about your values, goals, and ideas about creativity. It takes work to model creative thinking in action, but you don't have to be a creative genius. A terrific field-trip idea—or better, encouraging your students to think of one—is a good start. Students watch and respond to your example more than to your words. When teaching for creativity, the first rule is to remember that students follow what you do, not what you say. You can't simply talk the talk and expect results, you have to walk the walk.

Building Self–Efficacy

The main limitation on what students *can* do is what they think they *can't* do. All students have the capacity to be creators and to experience the joy associated with making something new, but first you must give them a strong base for creativity. Sometimes teachers and parents unintentionally limit what students can do by sending messages that express or imply limits on students' potential accomplishments.

Gratuitous advice kills both initiative and self-confidence and is often incorrect. Such advice may be overt or covert communication about a person not having the ability to do certain kinds of things, or the personality to do other kinds of things, or the motivation to complete something. Let your students know that they possess the ability to meet all of life's challenges—their job is to decide how hard they will work to meet the challenges.

Much—arguably most—of what we can't do in life is because we tell ourselves we can't (often because someone told us that we couldn't and we believed that person). Rosenthal and Jacobson (1968) told teachers that psychological testing revealed that some of their students were going to bloom during the next year. The randomly chosen potential bloomers did perform better than the other students, a result sometimes called the Pygmalion effect. Some investigators argue over details of the methodology used in the Rosenthal and Jacobson experiments, but few argue with the conclusions. Just setting an expectation is often enough to make it come true. Students can do pretty much whatever they make up their minds to do within natural limitations—what holds them back is a set of beliefs about their limitations.

We observed effects similar to those revealed by the Rosenthal and Jacobson experiments. Tommy was a big a problem in the 5th grade. His teacher complained about him constantly and bitterly. Tommy performed poorly academically, misbehaved in class, fought with other children, and talked back to the teacher. The teacher responded by frequently sending Tommy out of the class for remedial training, reasoning that Tommy didn't belong in a mainstream class because he lacked basic intelligence.

A remarkable thing happened to Tommy in 6th grade. His behavior, grades, and attendance improved. He stopped talking during class and interrupting the teacher, and he was rarely confrontational. He was a nicer kid and his appearance was neater and cleaner. Several factors were involved, but Tommy's new teacher was key to his transformation. At the start of the year, his 6th-grade teacher explained to us that she had been warned about a few children, especially Tommy. But she believed that Tommy's behavior problems prevented him from displaying academic competence. Tommy was verbal, as this teacher noted, and simply had to learn to use his oral skills for schoolwork.

While correcting Tommy's behavior, his 6th-grade teacher let him know that she felt he was capable of succeeding in school. When he performed poorly on a homework assignment, she explained to Tommy that he didn't have the preparation that the other students had experienced and that he should redo the task to develop his skills. She stopped sending him for remedial training because of the stigma associated with it. Instead, she worked with Tommy and let him know she believed in him. When the other children laughed at Tommy, the teacher pointed out that everyone makes mistakes. In defending him and allowing him to redo assignments, she made Tommy feel positive about himself. Tommy eventually proved capable of strikingly creative work, partly due to believing in himself. Recently Tommy announced to us that he loves school because he knows he can be good at it—quite a switch from 5th grade.

2 Learning Basic Techniques

*No artist is ahead of his time. He is his time. It is just
that others are behind the time.*

—Martha Graham

*Creativeness often consists of merely turning up
what is already there. Did you know that right and
left shoes were thought up only a little more than a
century ago?*

—Bernice Fitz-Gibbon

Questioning Assumptions

We all have assumptions. Often we don't know we have these
assumptions because they are widely shared. Creative people question
those assumptions and eventually lead others to do the same. When
Copernicus suggested that Earth revolves around the sun, the suggestion was viewed as preposterous because everyone could see that the
sun revolves around Earth. Galileo's ideas, including the relative rates of
falling objects, caused him to be banned as a heretic.

Sometimes it's not until many years later that the crowd realizes the
limitations or errors of their assumptions and the value of the creative
person's thoughts. The impetus of those who question assumptions
allow for cultural, technological, and other forms of advancement.

Teachers can be role models for questioning assumptions. You can
show students that what they assume they know, they don't really
know. Years ago, Sternberg's 7th-grade teacher asked the class if anyone did not know what *social studies* meant, and responded to our
silence by asking us what it meant. We spent two days examining, ques-

tioning, and changing assumptions about something we thought we knew. The discussion went far beyond mere definition, forcing us to question what social phenomena are and how we might study them.

Williams' high school teacher asked the class to list worthwhile career options for women and men on separate sides of the chalkboard. We volunteered answers typical for 1975. The teacher, a man, marveled at the number of answers we generated and then asked why certain occupations were on one side or the other. His question caused a bunch of 15-year-olds to think about our futures and what we might accomplish. By enabling us to make our assumptions explicit, the teacher focused our attention on the limitations imposed by the assumptions. The discussion allowed two boys to share their aspirations to become a chef and a dancer and three girls declared their intentions to try police work, brain surgery, and forestry. Twenty years later these ideas may not seem revolutionary or particularly creative, but this discussion encouraged us to question our assumptions before choosing a career.

Of course, students shouldn't question every assumption. There are times to question and then to try to reshape the environment and there are times to adapt to it. Some creative people question so many things so often that others stop taking them seriously. Everyone has to learn which assumptions are worth questioning and which battles are worth fighting. Sometimes it's better to leave the inconsequential assumptions alone so that you have an audience when you find something worth the effort.

Teaching students when to question and when not to is hard to communicate. How do you teach students what they should question and what they shouldn't, and how often to ask questions? Once on the creativity bus, younger students get into gear quickly and their zealous questions can be tough on their teachers and their parents. Now the children think of "better" ways to do everything. Some of the ideas may be good or interesting, but we must encourage questions without allowing the children to turn into monsters. How can you encourage an appropriate level of questioning in your students?

Make questioning a part of the daily classroom exchange. It's more important for students to learn what questions to ask—and how to ask them—than to learn the answers. Help your students evaluate their questions by discouraging the idea that you ask questions and they simply answer them. Avoid perpetuating the belief that your role is to teach students the facts. Instead, help the students understand that what matters is their ability to use facts. Help your students learn how to formulate good questions and how to answer questions.

We all tend to make a pedagogical mistake by emphasizing the answering and not the asking of questions. The good student is perceived as the one who rapidly furnishes the right answers. The expert in a field thus becomes the extension of the expert student—the one who knows and can recite a lot of information. As John Dewey (1933) recognized, *how* we think is often more important than *what* we think. We need to teach students how to ask the right questions (good, thought-provoking, and interesting ones) and lessen the emphasis on rote learning.

Students are natural questioners and use that skill to help them adapt to a changing complex environment. Whether your students continue to ask questions and challenge assumptions—and to ask good questions—depends largely on how you respond to their questions (Sternberg 1994). Knowing how to ask good questions is an essential part of intelligence and is possibly the most important part (Arlin 1990, Getzels and Csikszentmihalyi 1976, Sternberg 1985). It is an ability you can either foster or stifle.

When students ask questions, teachers respond in several different characteristic ways. How you respond to a question is differentially helpful in developing a student's intelligence. We propose a seven level model of teacher-student interaction in the questioning process (Sternberg 1994). Responses that correspond to the higher levels of our model better foster intellectual development than those in the lower levels. How you answer a student's question either places the student on the track to intellectual fulfillment or derailment. For example, after visiting Holland, seeing a documentary about Holland, or reading a book about the area, a student might ask why people in Holland are tall. Now consider the various ways you might respond to this or any question. The higher the level of your response, the more you enhance the student's intellectual development. Note that raising the level of response simply requires an affirming attitude toward the student and the question.

Level 1—Rejecting Questions. Typical responses include "don't ask so many questions," "don't bother me," "don't ask stupid questions," and "be quiet!" Responding in this manner sends the message that questions are inappropriate and irritating and students learn to be seen and not heard. Consistently punishing students for asking questions teaches them to stop asking questions and they learn less. Frustration, time constraints, and many other factors may push teachers to use these responses, but we must recognize the repercussions.

Level 2—Restating Questions as Responses. Typical responses are "because they are Dutch, and Dutch people are very tall," and "because they grow a lot." At this level we answer the question, but in a completely empty way. Our response is nothing more than a restatement of the original question. We state redundantly that people from Holland are tall because they are Dutch, or because the Dutch grow a lot. Or we say that a person acts the way he does "because he's human," or acts crazy "because she is insane," or that some people come up with good solutions "because they are high in intelligence."

Level 3—Admitting Ignorance or Responding Directly. Typical responses at this level are "I don't know" and "because [followed by a reasonable answer about nutrition or genetics]." At this level teachers either say they do not know or respond based on what they do know. Students are given the opportunity to learn something or to realize that their teachers do not know everything. Admitting ignorance or responding directly are reasonable answers in certain situations, but they are not the best responses for fostering learning.

Teachers can answer at this level either with or without a reward. A reward is "that's a good question," "I'm glad you asked that," or "that's a really interesting question." Such a response is likely to increase the frequency of questions and fosters more learning opportunities.

Level 4—Encouraging Information Seeking. Typical responses at this level are "I'll look it up in the encyclopedia" or "why don't you look it up in the encyclopedia?" Students learn that information can and should be sought and that the process does not end with just an answer or admission of ignorance.

Notice the difference in the two responses. In the first, the teacher takes responsibility for seeking the information and students learn that someone else will do the work for them. In the second response, the student is given the responsibility for learning and learns how to learn. Active learning helps students develop skills in seeking information.

Level 5—Considering Alternative Explanations. At this level the teacher admits ignorance and suggests ideas for the student to explore. Ideally, the student and teacher generate ideas together: People in Holland might be tall because of the food, weather, genetics, or hormone injections. The student learns that even simple questions invite formulating and testing hypotheses.

Level 6—Considering and Evaluating Explanations. Students are not only encouraged to explore alternative explanations, as in Level 5, but also to evaluate the explanations. A typical question is "how can we decide which of these explanations is correct?" For example, if genetics are responsible for the average height of the Dutch people, what do we expect to observe? How can we discern if food or weather is responsible? Students learn from the teacher's response not only how to generate alternative hypotheses, but also how to test hypotheses.

Level 7—Considering, Evaluating, and Following Up. A typical response is "let's gather some information we need to help us decide among these hypotheses." The teacher encourages the students to gather information that might help determine a valid hypothesis. The students learn how to think and how to act on their thoughts. Although it may not be possible to test every hypothesis, it is often possible to test several. For example, the students can gather information about whether taller Dutch parents tend to have taller children, or about the traditional Dutch diet.

ॐ ॐ ॐ

Note how the responses build from rejecting students' questions to encouraging the formulating and testing of hypotheses and from no learning to rote learning to analytic and creative learning. The higher level responses communicate interest in our students and their questions. Teachers don't have the time or resources to always respond in an ideal manner, nor are higher levels of response equally appropriate for all students—responses need to be developmentally appropriate. The more we use the higher levels as students grow up, however, the more we encourage and assist students in developing cognitive skills.

Defining and Redefining Problems

Promote creative performance by encouraging your students to define and redefine problems and projects. Encourage creative thinking by having students choose their own topics for papers or presentations, choose their own ways of solving problems, and sometimes choose again if they discover that their selection was a mistake. Allow your students to pick their own topics, subject to your approval, on at least one paper each term. Approval ensures that the topic is relevant to the lesson and has a chance of leading to a successful project.

A successful project (1) is appropriate to the course's goals, (2) illustrates a student's mastery of at least some of what has been taught, and (3) can earn a good grade. If a topic is so far from the goals that you will feel compelled to lower the grade, ask the student to choose another topic.

You can't always offer students choices, but giving choices is the only way for them to learn how to choose. A real choice is not deciding between drawing a cat or a cow, nor is it picking one state in the U.S.A. for the project fair. Give your students latitude in making choices to help them develop taste and good judgment, both essential elements of creativity.

Sometimes we all make mistakes in choosing a project or in the way we select to accomplish it. Just remember that an important part of creativity is the analytic part—learning to recognize a mistake. Give your students that chance and the opportunity to redefine their choices.

Encouraging Idea Generation

Once the problem is defined or redefined, it's time for students to generate ideas and solutions. In one of our research investigations, teachers assigned their classes a book report on colonial America. In most circumstances, the students would present an idea to the teacher a day or so later and would be off and running. What is wrong with this picture? A lot.

In this investigation, we encouraged teachers to state the general topic—colonial America—and then to distribute project planning sheets. The students spent two social studies class periods generating ideas for different types of projects and reports. Homework for those two nights was to come up with more ideas and to critique each one on the project planning sheet. For each idea students had to answer the following questions:

- What is the idea?

- What tools and materials are needed?

- How likely is a successful project?

- How much do you like the idea and why?

Together, the class explored the answers to the following questions:

- What types of ideas do most classmates prefer and why?

- What types of ideas are likely to lead to successful projects and why?

The volume of ideas generated was remarkable. Once the students got past their first few ideas, mostly ideas they had used in the past, the ideas became creative, challenging, and personally meaningful. One student's suggestion grew from a book report on *Uncle Tom's Cabin* into an accurate map and report on the Underground Railroad.

One student volunteered to write a report about food—growing, harvesting, storing, and cooking in colonial America, including recipes found in old books. He made three dishes with traditional ingredients for the class to taste while they debated the merits and pitfalls of mid-eighteenth century food practices. The report was creative, fresh, and was not among the first ideas on this student's list. He came up with the idea at home after participating in class discussion.

The environment for generating ideas must be relatively free of criticism. The students may acknowledge that some ideas are better or worse, but you must not be harsh or critical. Aim to identify and encourage any creative aspects of the ideas presented and suggest new approaches to any ideas that are simply uncreative. Praise your students for generating many ideas, regardless of whether some are silly or unrelated, while encouraging them to identify and develop their most unique ideas into high-quality projects.

Your students can use project planning in and out of school and in the future. Questions about marriage, family, and careers are best answered after thoroughly considering many ideas. Teaching students the value of generating numerous ideas enhances their creative-thinking ability and benefits them now and in the future.

Cross–Fertilizing Ideas

Stimulate creativity by helping students to think *across* subjects and disciplines. The traditional school environment often has separate classrooms and classmates for different subjects and seems to influence students into thinking that learning occurs in discrete boxes—the math box, the social studies box, and the science box. But creative ideas and insights often result from integrating material across subject areas, not from memorizing and reciting material.

Teaching students to cross-fertilize draws on their skills, interests, and abilities, regardless of the subject. For example, if your students are having trouble understanding math, you might ask them to draft test questions related to their special interests—ask the baseball fan to devise geometry problems based on the game. The context may spur creative ideas because the student finds the topic (baseball) enjoyable and it may counteract some of the anxiety caused by geometry. Cross-fertilization motivates students who aren't interested in subjects taught in the abstract.

One way to enact cross-fertilization in the classroom is to ask students to identify their best and worst academic areas. Then ask them to come up with project ideas in their weak area based on ideas borrowed from one of the strongest areas. Explain to them that they can apply their interest in science to social studies by analyzing the scientific aspects of trends in national politics. For example, opinion polling is often discussed in social studies, so help them link it to scientific reasoning by analyzing the pros and cons of opinion polling. Show your students techniques that are acceptable for conducting polls and techniques that render polls invalid. Then ask them to examine data predicting the results of upcoming local and national elections and to critique the pollster's predictions. Initiate a discussion about the media projecting results before the polls are closed.

Cross-fertilization helps students and teachers generate creative ideas for readings, reports, assignments, and assessments. For example, one student conducted a mock town poll about a referendum that would face the voters on election day. Another student clipped news articles referring to pollsters' predictions as guarantees and then explained why these predictions are invalid or at least unwise. Use cross-fertilization techniques in teaching, "how can we think about this physics problem? How about thinking about Michael Jordan playing baseball versus Michael Jordan playing basketball. What can we learn that's relevant to this physics problem?" Suddenly all of the basketball and baseball lovers are interested in solving that physics problem.

3 Teaching Tips

When in doubt, make a fool of yourself. There is a microscopically thin line between being brilliantly creative and acting like the most gigantic idiot on earth. So what the hell, leap.

—*Cynthia Heimel*

I just invent, then wait until people come around to needing what I've invented.

—*R. Buckminster Fuller*

Allowing Time for Creative Thinking

Ours is a society in a hurry. We eat fast food, we rush from one place to another, and we value quickness. Indeed, one way to say someone is smart is to say that the person is quick (Sternberg 1985), a square indication of our values. Just take a look at the format of our standardized tests—lots of multiple choice problems squeezed into a brief time slot.

Most creative insights, however, do not happen in a flash (Gruber 1986). We need time to understand a problem and to toss it around. If we are asked to think creatively, we need time to do it well. If you stuff questions into exams or give your students more homework than they can complete, then you are not allowing them time to think creatively.

Teachers in the United States have substantially less free time than in Japan (Stevenson and Stigler 1992). The result is that the teachers, like the students, scarcely have any time to think. If you want your students to develop creative thinking skills, you need to give them the time to do so.

After you assign a paper or a report, or after you ask a complex question, give your students a thinking session of 10 minutes or more (depending on their ages and your needs). Introduce this technique to your students by explaining that they must use the time to think carefully, openly, and creatively about a particular problem. Do not interrupt them during this time or cut the time short. Let your students know that the time is for pondering and thinking and that they may not engage in any other activity.

Is it a waste of time to encourage students to sit and think and list options before choosing one to pursue in an essay or report? No. Contemplation raises the quality of the final product and helps students plan for completing the project from the start. You can expect fewer nasty surprises and unexpected glitches because tasks are better planned. Ultimately, making the time to teach students the value of contemplation raises the quality of work and makes assignments more productive and fulfilling learning experiences.

The idea is to help your students develop the discipline necessary for creative thinking. Giving homework that allows and encourages them to take the time to think helps them get used to the time it takes to develop a creative idea. Allow time for creative thoughts as you determine the time they need to complete a test, essay, or assignment. By building in time for pondering, you show students that time spent thinking is valuable. Creative ideas depend on nurturing the inklings that lead to these ideas, and nurturing creative ideas requires time.

Instructing and Assessing Creatively

If you only give multiple-choice tests, students quickly learn the type of thinking that you value, no matter what you say. If you want to encourage creativity, you need to include at least some opportunities for creative thought in assignments and tests. Ask questions that require factual recall, analytic thinking, *and* creative thinking. For example, ask your students to identify the basic tenets of theories of government and to synthesize and integrate them with their own ideas to produce a new theory. You won't receive publishable new theories or answers, but you can expect your students to practice creative thinking.

The same principle can be applied to any course. In English, ask your students to write short stories, poems, or alternative endings to familiar stories. In social studies, ask your students to pretend to be a great individual in history and to make and defend a decision on a critical question faced by that person. In science, ask them to propose intuitive theories of phenomena, to design simple experiments, or to do independent research projects. In mathematics, ask them to invent word problems, systems of enumeration, or measurement. In foreign language class, students can create skits that simulate the language and culture being studied. The only limitations in the assignment are those set by the imaginations of the teacher and students.

Do not limit creativity to written assignments. Students won't try creative thinking unless you ask stimulating questions in class, so don't wait for tests or papers. Encourage your students to think creatively by asking them to imagine, suppose, create, invent, hypothesize, and speculate whenever you can.

Any time you ask your students to go beyond the information given, you offer them an opportunity to be creative. Consider the following types of questions that span a range of topics:

- Imagine you are an Inuit fisherman. How do you feel about the Canadian government's plan to build a road, linking your village with a larger village 50 miles away?

- Suppose the military asks you to build the first atomic bomb. What do you do?

- Create a new ending to *The Secret Sharer* by Joseph Conrad and explain why your ending makes sense in the context of the plot.

- Invent and describe a device that prevents car theft.

- Hypothesize about why so many politicians are also lawyers.

- Speculate about why so many words in English and Spanish are similar.

Rewarding Creative Ideas and Products

It's not enough to talk about the value of creativity: You have to reward it. Students are used to authority figures who say one thing and do another. They are exquisitely sensitive to what teachers value when it comes to the bottom line, namely, the grade or evaluation. If you do not put your money where your mouth is, they'll go with the money—that is, the grade.

Reward creative efforts. For example, assign a project and remind students that you are looking for them to demonstrate their knowledge, analytical and writing skills, and creativity. Let them know that creativity does not depend on your agreement with what they write, only that they express ideas that represent a synthesis between existing ideas and their own thoughts. You need to care only that the ideas are creative from the students' perspectives, not necessarily creative with regard to the state-of-the-art. Students may generate an idea that someone else has already had.

Some teachers complain that they cannot grade creative responses with as much objectivity as they can apply to multiple-choice or short-answer responses. They are correct in that there is some sacrifice of objectivity; however, research shows that evaluators are remarkably consistent in their assessments of creativity (Amabile 1983, Sternberg and Lubart 1995). If the goal of assessment is to instruct students, then it's better to ask for creative work and evaluate it with somewhat less objectivity than to evaluate students on uncreative work. Let your students know that there is no completely objective way to evaluate creativity.

Consider encouraging the growth and development of creativity in your students by giving a separate creativity grade. The standard overall grade of an assignment does reflect creative content, but it also encompasses accuracy, comprehensiveness, style, and grammar. How you use creativity grades in final class grading is your decision. The point is that the separate grade explicitly rewards the creative process and effort, regardless of the quality of the overall assignment.

In our research on teaching practical and creative intelligence to 5th- and 6th-graders (Williams, Blythe, White, Sternberg, Li, and Gardner 1996), we found that defining specific measures of creative performance enables teachers to be more receptive and encouraging of students' creativity. These teachers were able to focus on creativity as an essential ingredient of a good assignment because they knew that they were to grade assignments for creative content. Teachers avoided discouraging students who were learning the creative process by opting to comment "a bit creative" or "could be more creative" as the lowest grade.

The teachers reported that they and their students benefited from explicitly recognizing creative performance—whether through grades, classroom demonstrations, votes from their peers, or other special recognition. To encourage student creativity, you must identify, nurture, and reward it. Students are often discouraged from focusing on creativity in their assignments and discussions. It's the job of good teachers to reward creativity, especially considering the role it plays both inside and outside of school.

4 Avoiding Roadblocks

In creating, the only hard thing's to begin; a grass blade's no easier to make than an oak.

—*James Russell Lowell*

People are like trees: each one must put forth the leaf that is created in him.

—*Henry Ward Beecher*

Encouraging Sensible Risks

Creative people take risks and defy the crowd by buying low and selling high. Defying the crowd means risking the crowd's wrath. But there are sensible—and less sensible—reasons to defy the crowd. Creative people take sensible risks and produce ideas that others ultimately admire and respect as trendsetting. In taking these risks, yes, creative people sometimes make mistakes, fail, and fall flat on their faces.

We emphasize *sensible* risk-taking, because we are not talking about risking life and limb. We are talking about the kinds of risks taken by Monet, Picasso, Shakespeare, and Dostoyevsky when they influenced how we think about art and literature. Although few, if any, of our students will become great artists, you can help them develop their creative potentials.

To help students learn to take sensible risks, encourage them to take some intellectual risks—with courses, activities, and teachers—to develop a sense of how to assess risks. Research shows that creative children and adults take intellectual risks (Sternberg and Lubart 1991). Although not every intellectual activity should be a risk, risks increase the chances that a person is likely to do creative work or work that makes a difference—for that person and perhaps for others. Most creative work goes at least slightly against the established way of doing things and the results are not always positive: A student summons the courage to take a difficult course and fails, or writes a provocative and controversial essay and receives a bad grade, or chooses an offbeat science project and doesn't win a prize.

Then why encourage students to take risks? Nearly every major discovery or invention entailed some risk. When a movie theater was the only place to see a movie, someone created the idea of the home video industry: Skeptics wondered if anyone would want to see videos on a small screen. Another initially risky idea was the home computer: Would anyone have enough use for a home computer to justify the cost? These ideas were once risks that are now ingrained in our society.

Clifford (1988) studied how students' willingness to take academic risks influenced their development and performance. The study shows that tolerance for failure at school is associated with choosing certain levels of test problems. Students who tolerate failure take greater risks and choose harder problems. Tolerance for failure was also associated with higher standardized achievement test scores. However, tolerance for failure decreases with age—the older the children, the more society has influenced them to play it safe.

Given the learning opportunities that derive from taking risks and the achievement that learning makes possible, why are so few children willing to take risks in school? That's easy. Perfect test scores and papers receive praise; failure means extra work. Failure to attain a certain academic standard is perceived as a lack of ability and motivation rather than as reflecting a desire to grow. Teachers advocate playing it safe by giving assignments without choices and expecting specific answers to questions.

Unfortunately, students and adults averse to taking risks lose in the end. Children naturally take risks and feel a certain invulnerability until society teaches them otherwise. We must become aware of the many subtle ways in which parents, teachers, and other members of society discourage us from taking risks. We must try to balance appropriate caution with sensible risks.

Schools, for the most part, discourage taking risks. Children learn early how the system of schooling works: To succeed you need good grades, and to get good grades you can't take chances. You need those grades to get into better sections, to be admitted to advanced courses, to get into college, and to get into advanced training or the best job stream. Just a few risks or a few low grades can put you out of the running for the greatest advancement and best placement.

We observed 3rd-grade children as their teacher introduced a lesson on the planets. The teacher explained that they were to imagine being astronauts by dressing up and pretending to fly to Mars. Sara suggested that she dress up as a Martian and meet the astronauts on Mars. The teacher immediately told Sara that she couldn't do that because space probes indicate that there are no Martians. The effect of the teacher's response on Sara had nothing to do with Martians or space probes. Sara risked suggesting an interesting and creative idea and was shot down. The teacher's reaction was a result of limited time for a planned lesson—time that might have been used to encourage students to explore creative ideas. As teachers, we need to be careful lest our desire to stay on track and on time causes our students to learn that thinking creatively and taking risks means getting shot down.

It's no wonder that it is so much easier to observe creativity in young children than in older children and adults. By encouraging intellectual risk-taking you can unleash creative potential in your students and in yourself. Encouraging risk-taking means rewarding it. If a student takes a sensible risk in choosing a paper topic or a point of view, encourage it even if you need to give mixed feedback on the product. You can compliment the risk while showing ways in which the process or the product might be improved: "That was an unusual and exciting topic for a book report, Kyle. But maybe you could have done a bit more to show why the military thought it was important to train dolphins to carry and plant explosives."

Tolerating Ambiguity

People like things to be in black and white. We like to think that a country is good or bad (ally or enemy) or that a given idea in education works or doesn't work. The problem is that there are a lot of grays in creative work. Artists working on new paintings and writers working on new books often report feeling depressed and scattered in their thoughts: "Do I really like this subject and this approach after all? What about the first idea I had—that might have worked out better! I don't like the way this is turning out. I should go back to the idea I had two weeks ago and redo what I've done since." After resolving the issues, the idea will have its pluses and minuses and it's rare for the creator to feel that a product is perfect.

Part of the reason everyone needs time to be creative is that a creative idea tends to come in bits and pieces and develops over time. But the period in which the idea is developing tends to be uncomfortable. Without time or the ability to tolerate ambiguity, you may jump to a less than optimal solution.

Linus Pauling didn't discover the structure of DNA because he did not tolerate ambiguity quite long enough. He published a helical structure that provided Francis Crick and James Watson some of the pieces they needed to complete their work. Many times a company releases a product before polishing it and allows another company to enter the market soon afterward with the perfected idea—and win the sales.

Tolerating ambiguity is uncomfortable. When a student has almost the right topic for a paper, or almost the right science project, it's tempting to accept the near-miss. To help students become creative, encourage them to accept and extend the period in which their ideas don't quite converge. We observed an English class in which Alex was trying to write a creative poem to read to the class. One student wrote a poem from the perspective of a bird flying over the town. The class loved it. Another student wrote a poem about how colors in the sunset might taste. Again, the class loved it. Alex struggled to write about baseball, but his teacher said that his drafts looked like the same old baseball poem. Alex became increasingly uncomfortable as his classmates read their poems, but the teacher insisted on a creative approach.

Although more than half of the students read their poems before lunch, Alex didn't have an approach until that afternoon. He decided to write about the baseball field on the day of a world series game, from sunrise through the separate arrivals of the stadium workers, players, and fans. The final verse was about the empty field that night, strewn with candy wrappers and drink cups. Each of the six verses of Alex's poem described a different phase of the day and elicited a different feeling from the audience. Alex tolerated ambiguity for what felt like eons until producing a high quality project and experiencing the reward.

Encourage your students to see the ambiguity in situations and to appreciate it, and show them that the process allows us to reach better and more thoughtful conclusions. Use an exercise to demonstrate how ambiguity feels by asking the class to ponder a tough question, perhaps a current social or political concern. For example, should the United States be involved in a particular military conflict? Or, should vitamins be treated and regulated as drugs? Whatever the area and question, suppress any tendency to help the students come to rapid closure and insist that they argue more than one side of the issue. Use the statements to begin group discussions or as the basis for essays, homework assignments, or questions on an exam.

Another way to approach the experience of ambiguity is by sharing biographical materials on famous scientists, artists, and other great creators. Show students that contemplation enables them to formulate creative ideas and that ambiguity is often preparation for generating creative work.

Allowing Mistakes

Buying low and selling high carries a danger. Many ideas are unpopular simply because they aren't good. People often think a certain way because that way works better than other ways. But once in a while a great thinker comes along—a Freud, a Piaget, a Chomsky, or an Einstein—and shows us a new way to think. These thinkers made contributions because they allowed themselves and their collaborators to take risks and make mistakes.

Many of Freud's and Piaget's ideas are wrong. Freud confused Victorian issues regarding sexuality with universal conflicts and Piaget misjudged the ages at which children could perform certain cognitive feats. Their ideas were great *not* because they lasted forever, but because they became the basis for other ideas. Freud's and Piaget's mistakes allowed others to profit from the ideas and go beyond.

Schools are often unforgiving of mistakes. Errors on schoolwork are often marked with a large and pronounced *X*. When children respond to questions with incorrect answers, some teachers pounce on the students for not having read or understood the material and other students snicker. When children go outside the lines in the coloring book, or use a different color, they are corrected. In hundreds of ways and in thousands of instances over the course of a school career, children learn that it's not OK to make mistakes. The result is that they become afraid to risk the independent and the sometimes flawed thinking that leads to creativity.

Sometimes a response seems like a mistake only because it doesn't fit the teacher's point of view. Several years ago we observed a class in which the teacher asked the children who discovered America. A child blurted out, "the Indians." Everyone laughed, and the teacher hastened to correct the mistake, naming Christopher Columbus. Before correcting a response, we need to make sure that it needs to be corrected.

Remember that part of encouraging students to be creative is to help them gain confidence in their ability to generate lots of ideas. Anyone who generates many ideas is going to have some poor ideas and make mistakes. Did you know that baseball's king of home runs, Babe Ruth, also held the strike-out record? We don't remember him this way, do we? Society focuses on the accomplishments of creative and talented people and forgets and forgives the mistakes. Although we all make mistakes, artists are remembered for their best compositions, scientists for their greatest ideas. Teach your students that everyone makes mistakes and that the only thing wrong with making reasonable and defensible mistakes is failing to profit from them.

When your students make mistakes, ask them to analyze and discuss these mistakes. Often, mistakes or weak ideas contain the germ of correct answers or good ideas. In Japan, teachers spend entire class periods asking children to analyze the mistakes in their mathematical thinking. For the teacher who wants to make a difference, exploring mistakes can be a learning and growing opportunity.

Identifying and Surmounting Obstacles

Creative people always encounter obstacles. It's the nature of the enterprise—the crowd does not welcome defiance. As a new assistant professor, I gave a talk at a testing organization believing that they would welcome new ideas about intelligence. Hardly! They had a vested interest in a certain kind of test based on certain notions of intelligence, and were far from receptive to hearing that their edifice was incorrect. Similarly, pharmaceutical companies with their multi-million dollar investments in antacids did not embrace the scientists who proposed that antacid drugs don't counteract ulcers, only stomach acids.

Creative thinkers almost inevitably encounter resistance. The question is whether the creative thinker has the fortitude to persevere. We understand why so many young and promising creative thinkers disappear. Sooner or later, they decide that being creative isn't worth the resistance and punishment. The truly creative thinkers pay the short-term price because they recognize that they can make a difference.

Describe obstacles that you, friends, and famous people have faced while trying to be creative; otherwise your students may think that obstacles confront only them. Include stories about people who weren't supportive, bad grades for unwelcome ideas, and cool receptions to your ideas. To help your students deal with obstacles, remind them of the many creative people whose ideas were initially shunned and help them develop an inner sense of awe of the creative act. You can suggest that they reduce their concern over what others think, but it's tough for adolescents to lessen their dependence on their peers.

When you can, praise and encourage students for accomplishment as well as for effort. When a student attempts to surmount an obstacle, praise the effort whether or not the student is entirely successful. Point out aspects of the student's attack that were successful and why, then suggest other ways to confront similar obstacles. You can also tactfully critique counterproductive approaches by describing a better approach as long as you praise the attempt. Ask the class to brainstorm about ways to confront a given obstacle to get them thinking about the many strategies we can use to confront problems. Consider the student who has always been too nervous to act in school plays or to sing a solo. Spend a half hour asking students to generate strategies for dealing with performance anxiety and to chronicle personal examples that show how nervousness can be disabling. List ideas on the board and ask the class to critique them. Encourage students to try a couple of the strategies and praise them for any attempts at overcoming performance anxiety. The emphasis on tackling obstacles should help students focus on solving problems instead of being limited by them.

5 Adding Complex Techniques

Creativity is so delicate a flower that praise tends to make it bloom, while discouragement often nips it in the bud. Any of us will put out more and better ideas if our efforts are appreciated.

—*Alex F. Osborn*

The best way to have a good idea is to have lots of ideas.

—*Linus Pauling*

Teaching Self-Responsibility

Part of teaching students to be creative is teaching them to take responsibility for both success and failure. Teaching students how to take responsibility means teaching students to (1) understand their creative process, (2) criticize themselves, and (3) take pride in their best creative work. Unfortunately, many teachers and parents look for—or allow students to look for—an outside enemy responsible for failures.

It sounds trite to say that you should teach students to take responsibility for themselves. But sometimes there is a gap between what we know and how we translate thought into action. In practice, people differ widely in the extent to which they take responsibility for the causes and consequences of their actions. Rotter (1966) distinguished between two personality patterns, internal and external. Internals take responsibility for their lives and when things go well, they take credit; when things don't go well, they take responsibility and try to make it better. Externals place responsibility outside themselves, especially when things do not go well. They are quick to blame circumstances for their failures and often attribute successes to external circumstances. Of course, almost no one is purely internal or external. We all know people who accept credit for successes and blame others for failures, or people who do not credit themselves for successes and blame themselves for failures. Realistic people recognize that both success and failure come about as an interaction between their own contributions and the contributions of others.

As researchers studying how to maximize intellectual potential, we found that people who tend toward the internal side of the continuum are better adapted to intellectual success (Rotter 1966, Sternberg 1986, Williams et al. 1996). Externals are reluctant or refuse to accept blame and do not take responsibility for making the most of their lives. Our observations of students at Yale reveal that one of the best predictors of success is the individual's willingness to take responsibility. Most of the students who attend Yale are used to success—and many wait for something to happen. The students who succeed *make* their opportunities and take responsibility for their lives.

Help develop responsibility in your students by serving as a role model. Students learn through imitating modeled behaviors and won't take responsibility for themselves if you seek to blame someone else for your problems—other teachers, administrators, the government, or the students. These entities may be in part responsible for the problems, but you must demonstrate efforts toward improving the situation.

Another way to help students develop a sense of responsibility is to know when *not* to push students. Students who have been pushed by their parents face college—and other situations—not knowing how to push themselves. The most successful students have been nudged when circumstances required it, but were not constantly pushed throughout childhood.

Intellectually successful people are not those who do just enough to get by. As teachers, we see many students who do only what they think is necessary to get an *A*, *B*, or whatever grade they set as a goal. Although they may get the grade, these students are not taking responsibility for their lives. Children who learn to get by behave the same way as adults and nearly always someone else gets the choice opportunities in life.

Teach your students to take responsibility and to translate thought into action because there is often a gap between what we know how to do and what we actually do. We see scholars who have good ideas, but who never get around to publishing them. We see inventors who have creative ideas, but procrastinate until someone else markets the idea. We see managers hesitate to make changes until the company goes into bankruptcy. And, we have all seen people in relationships who know that changes need to be made, but who wait until they've lost the relationship. To make the most of our abilities, it's not enough to learn what to do—we have to learn to do it.

Promoting Self-Regulation

You can't help each student during each creative process. Your students must take control of the process. After forming initial creative products and awakening the joy of creating in your students, teach them strategies for self-regulation. Self-directed creating is how most of us work throughout our lives—and especially in our lives outside of school.

How do you know when you're onto something good? How can you tell if you're spending too much time on something that may not amount to much in terms of a creative product? How can you decide which idea to pursue? And how can you benefit from self-appraisal and feedback from others? Ann Brown and her colleagues did research on how to teach students self-regulation skills (Brown, Bransford, Ferrara, and Campione 1983). They advocate a three-step method for teaching strategies: (1) teach the strategy and explain it clearly, giving practical examples of when and how to use it; (2) encourage students to evaluate the tangible gains that using the strategy will bring about; and (3) instruct students to remind themselves to use the strategy.

Consider our research on teaching practical and creative intelligence for school (Williams et al. 1996). We wanted to teach students strategies for self-regulation to help them (1) choose the right questions and ideas; (2) plan how to proceed with their writing, reports, and projects; (3) stay on track and maintain their motivation; and (4) evaluate their performance.

After the project was complete, the student and teacher evaluated the grade and comments together. After that, students graded each other's assignments and exchanged feedback. Discussing feedback encouraged high-quality products. Upon completing the exercise, which took time each day for several days, the teachers asked the students what they learned from the process that would be valuable for the next report. The emphasis was on learning strategies the students could use to self-regulate during the creative process. The following process resulted from the experience and feedback:

1. List multiple ideas for an assignment
2. Assess ideas for creativity and pursue one
3. Defend your choice
4. Develop plans for completing the assignment, including how and where to find information, and how and when you will finish the project
5. Keep a daily log of progress, roadblocks, and how you surmounted problems
6. Participate in daily class discussions regarding progress on the report and physical distractions (being hungry or tired)
7. Discuss teacher feedback on finished projects
8. Assess a classmate's project and review and discuss peer evaluations

The emphasis on the *process* of completing a project—from the initial idea through peer reactions—helped students develop an appreciation of the many steps involved in high-quality, creative work.

The task of enhancing creativity is a tough one. An essential aspect is to remember that creativity is self-driven, therefore the strategies for controlling the process must come from the individual. In other research we found that teaching metacognitive strategies caused real gains in intellectual performance versus uninstructed controls (Davidson and Sternberg 1984, Sternberg 1987). As students learn and grow during the process of learning to create, they must also learn how to monitor and regulate their creative process.

Delaying Gratification

Part of being creative means being able to work on a project or task for a long time without immediate or interim rewards. Students must learn rewards aren't always immediate and that there are benefits to delaying gratification.

Many people believe that they should reward children immediately for good performance, and that children should expect rewards. This style of teaching and parenting emphasizes the here and now and often comes at the expense of what's best in the long term.

An important lesson in life—and one that is intimately related to developing the discipline to do creative work—is to learn to wait for rewards. The greatest rewards are often those that are delayed. Give your students examples of delayed gratification in your life and in the lives of creative individuals and help them apply these examples to their lives.

In a series of studies spanning many years, Walter Mischel has found that children who delay gratification are more successful in various aspects of their lives, including academic performance (Mischel, Shoda, and Rodriguez 1989). In a typical study, Mischel places young children in a room and gives them a choice between an immediate reward and a later, larger reward. He puts various temptations in their paths. For example, it is harder to resist if the immediate reward (a chocolate bar) is visible than if it is hidden. Interestingly, children's ability to delay gratification indicates how they will score on the *Scholastic Assessment Test* when they are much older.

Howard Gruber's life work is to study the careers of the world's great contributors (Gruber 1986). His findings belie the notion that the great insights in history result from flashes of understanding. Gruber has found that the greatest minds worked hard and long to achieve their great accomplishments and to complete their major works.

The work of Ericsson, Krampe, and Tesch-Römer (1993) suggests that an important factor in becoming an expert in anything is hard work and practice. Comparisons of distinguished performers in several fields with those who are not so distinguished reveal that the distinguished performers worked much harder and in a more focused, deliberate way. Hard work on one pursuit represents a risk because there is no guarantee that the hard work will yield results. A child may practice for hours and hours and never become a great hockey player, artist, or violinist. Yet, the work of Ericsson and colleagues suggests that few things pay off as much as persistence and determination.

Hard work does not often bring immediate rewards. Children do not immediately become expert baseball players, dancers, musicians, or sculptors. And the reward of becoming an expert seems far away. Children often succumb to the temptations of the moment—watching television or playing video games. The people who make the most of their abilities are those who wait for a reward and recognize that few serious challenges are met in a moment. Ninth-grade students may not see the benefits of hard work, but the advantages of a solid academic performance will be obvious when those students apply to college.

The short-term focus of most school assignments does little to teach children the value of delaying gratification. Projects are clearly superior in meeting this goal, but it is difficult to assign home projects if you aren't confident of parental involvement and support. In a nonsupportive environment, maintain a focus on projects by spending class time on the projects. No matter where the project is done, the student plays the significant role in planning the project, choosing the topic and format of presentation, and determining the steps involved in completing it. By working on a task for many weeks or months, a student learns the value of making incremental efforts for long-term gains.

One 5th grader, Ginny, hadn't been taught much at home about delaying gratification. Her parents worked long hours and ameliorated their guilt by indulging Ginny with toys and treats. She was naturally gifted academically and consequently never had to push to get good grades. Fortunately, Ginny's 5th-grade teacher knew that ability without perseverance does not guarantee success. The teacher assigned long-term projects that required stamina and patience to help the students develop these qualities.

Ginny's teacher assigned the class three long-term projects and required daily journal entries. The ideas for the projects were from self-generated lists. As a result of these assignments Ginny learned patience and persistence. We do children a disservice by hurrying to provide them with immediate rewards because the real world doesn't work that way.

6 Using Role Models

Creative intelligence in its various forms and activities is what makes man.

—*James Harvey Robinson*

Using Profiles of Creative People

Research shows that people, even 4-year-old children, often engage in *case-based reasoning* (Hammond 1990, Riesbeck and Schank 1989), meaning that people learn and understand information by studying specific examples of other people and situations. Integrate that idea with stories of creative people and their situations. For example, tell your students the story of how a child came to the point of inventing a nationally sold device for cooking bacon to a crisp in a microwave oven. The story can help your students understand the pitfalls and triumphs of bringing creative ideas to fruition, and exposure to multiple and varied examples can have a highly positive impact on the acquisition of conceptual knowledge (Druckman and Bjork 1991, Smith and Medin 1981). Case-based learning argues for the relevance and appropriateness of using individual cases or profiles in instructing students in creativity.

Select material that contains information about (1) the problems and related concepts, (2) the procedures used to solve the problem, and (3) how the components of the case are related. Case knowledge has a long-term impact on thinking (Fivush, Hudson, and Nelson 1984). For example, kindergarten children who went to a museum of archaeology were asked about that particular trip (later that day, six weeks later, and one year later) and their memories about trips to other museums. The children's memories of the museum of archaeology did not include intrusions from the script they had about trips to museums in general, offering evidence that children retain experiences as specific memories and not as one big concept. After six years these children still did not confuse the archaeology museum trip with their general notions about museum trips (Hudson and Fivush 1991, Wagenaar 1986).

To develop creativity, this research suggests that introducing profiles of creative people and their experiences gives students powerful information that exists independently and complements previously stored information. For example, students often think that the way to come up with a topic for a paper is to choose a topic that the teacher is likely to reward with an *A* (it's a bonus if it interests the student). After reading a profile of a writer who chose nontraditional topics, however, students might be better able to select an offbeat and creative topic to write about. For example, information about Walt Whitman's free-form verse and commonplace subjects might inspire students to write about interesting daily topics and to shed the notion that poems must rhyme.

You can help students use the strategies illustrated in the examples to stimulate creative abilities by prompting them when you give assignments: "How would Walt Whitman have approached this assignment? Think about his method of choosing a topic and think about what it meant to his writing before choosing your topic."

To make the case-based method work in teaching creativity, present the profiles and examples together with explanations that help students understand the situation as a whole and the interrelationship of its parts (Chen and Daehler 1989, 1992). In our Whitman example, describe Whitman's character and experiences and the challenges of writing poetry in a new way. Your students won't always use the procedural knowledge they gain from an example (Gick and Holyoak 1980, 1983; Reed 1989), but they are more likely to use richly presented examples.

Choose cases interesting and relevant to the subject matter—perhaps a profile of a creative scientist for biology class, or a famous poet in English class, or a great explorer for a social studies lesson. Discuss a pivotal point in the person's life to help your students identify with the creator and internalize the lesson. Later, remind students of the value of applying these lessons by pointing out parallels between the situations faced by great creators and the situations all of us face from time to time—including few ringing endorsements of our ideas. Draw the link between daily work and the great ideas of talented creators.

Encouraging Creative Collaboration

Creative performance is often viewed as a solitary occupation—we picture the writer sitting alone with her pad, the artist painting maniacally at 4 a.m., and the musician playing for his cats into the wee hours. In reality, people often work in groups and collaboration can spur creativity. Encourage your students to collaborate with creative people because we all learn by example. Students benefit from seeing the techniques, strategies, and approaches that others use in the creative process. Also, students absorb the enthusiasm and joy many creative people exude as they go about the business of making something new.

Finding practical ways to encourage creative performance from groups of students is essential because you can't work with students one-on-one all of the time. Since life involves working with others, it's worthwhile to make the process of collaboration more creative.

Research shows that students prefer learning through collaborative discussion (Thorkildsen 1989, 1991). Cognitive development is likely to be profoundly influenced by group dialogue on content issues as each student absorbs and benefits from group discussions and experiences substantial learning in the process (Vygotsky 1978). Research shows the omnipresence of collaborative thinking in our society (Resnick, Levine, and Teasley 1991; Schrage 1990); therefore we need to make these collaborations generate more creative work.

Enhance collaborative creativity by asking each student to generate an idea, to describe it briefly to a small group (about five members), and then to continue generating ideas for a prescribed length of time. The groups can discuss the ideas as you model an accepting attitude and discourage critical responses. You can help establish the right dynamic by rewarding the groups for the sheer volume of ideas as well as for high-quality, creative ideas. Stress good ideas as the goal and explain why some ideas are better than others, while encouraging your students to generate ideas without worrying about criticism. Encourage other creative collaborations by asking groups of students to write artistic compositions, songs, and plays—each student can develop and describe characters or have some role in the final product.

Diversify creative collaborations by inviting adult creators into your classroom to discuss their work and encourage students to find, work with, and watch creative people in their free time. Adult role models help students think about the value of a creative mind-set outside of school.

Imagining Other Viewpoints

An essential aspect of working with other people and getting the most out of collaborative creative activity is to imagine ourselves in other people's shoes. We broaden our perspective by learning to see the world from a different point of view, and that experience enhances our creative ability and contributions. Spur creative work by facing new and unexpected situations.

Encourage your students to see the importance of understanding, respecting, and responding to other people's points of view. Many bright and potentially creative children never achieve success because they do not develop practical intelligence (Sternberg 1985, 1988b). They may do well in school and on tests, but they never learn how to get along with others or to see things and themselves as others see them. Girls are better able to imagine someone else's point of view and tend to be more sensitive to and understanding of feelings than boys (Hall 1984). Thus, we need to pay special attention to these issues with boys because understanding another person's viewpoint allows students to more easily adapt to the demands of school and life.

It's not enough to understand other viewpoints. Our actions must reflect this understanding. Few things impede intellectual development and creative performance more than defensiveness against other viewpoints or criticism. Some people don't want to hear anyone else's opinion and if they do, they immediately assume it is wrong—or tune it out.

When a teacher criticizes a student, the student's first reaction may be that the teacher must be wrong. As teachers, we should be the first to admit that we can be wrong. But students need to learn to do the same thing we should do—think about the criticisms, consider the source or sources, and only then decide to accept or reject the criticism. Chances are that the criticism contains something the student can use to an advantage.

One particularly bright but stubborn pupil illustrated this phenomenon for us recently. Bruce was extremely capable academically, but he did not get along with anybody. Bruce thought he was always right, and we could see where he got this attitude: His parents reinforced his beliefs. Parent-teacher conferences were frustrating—not even the principal could explain to Bruce's parents that he had trouble getting along with others.

Bruce was the loser in this situation because he didn't develop the ability to see things from another person's viewpoint. He didn't have close friends and his sister couldn't tolerate him. He was trained to ignore criticism and thus never improved himself in response to feedback. Bruce is now in middle school and is learning to behave tactfully, get along with others, and make a reasonable impression on others. He is becoming an adolescent and truly wants to make friends and fit in with his peer group.

Growing up helped Bruce change. And, feeling like an outcast in all group situations reinforced what his teachers were telling him—that he needs to get along with others. Bruce transcended his own perspective by developing an appreciation for what other people felt and thought. By broadening his perspective and relaxing his self-righteousness, Bruce opened up space inside for creative ideas to begin to germinate.

7 Exploring the Environment

I must create a system or be enslaved by another man's.

—William Blake

Recognizing Environmental Fit

The next strategy is one that is as important to the teacher as it is to the student. It stems from the fact that creativity is not really objective. What is judged as creative is an interaction between a person and the environment (Csikszentmihalyi 1988, Gardner 1993, Sternberg and Lubart 1995). The very same product that is rewarded as creative in one time or place may be scorned in another.

In *The Dead Poets' Society*, a teacher whom the audience might well judge to be creative is viewed as incompetent by the school's staff. Similar experiences occur many times a day in many settings. There is no absolute standard for what constitutes creative work because the same lesson, school-reform idea, or product may be valued or scoffed in different environments. The lesson is that we need to find a setting in which our creative talents and unique contributions are rewarded or we need to modify our environment.

Some environments and expectations are not a good fit for a person's creative abilities. Reinforce this lesson for students who find that other teachers, students, and their parents do not support their growing creative talents. Ask your students to contemplate what they have to offer creatively. Don't let them stop with only a few ideas and suggestions—really get them thinking about their goals and talents. Now discuss the environment in which best to nurture their goals. Mention that the right environment unleashes the creative spirit and makes accomplishments possible. Ask your students about environments they have experienced that do not foster creative development or achievement.

While discussing the future, mention the notion of person-environment fit. Stress that one college, one town, one basketball team, or one art class may be right and another may be wrong. Help your students understand that a teacher and class that they love might alienate their friends. Point out that many great artists, composers, and other creative geniuses have worked to shape their environments to their creative needs or have found new environments. Remind your students that we all have unique environmental needs. By building a constant appreciation of the person-environment fit, you prepare your students for choosing environments that are conducive to their creative success. Encourage your students to examine environments to help them learn to select and match environments with their abilities.

Finding Excitement

To unleash your students' best creative performances, you must help them find what excites them. Remember that it may not be what really excites you nor what you wish would really excite them. Don't try to influence your students, but help them match their abilities, interests, and opportunities.

People who truly excel in a pursuit, whether vocational or avocational, almost always genuinely love what they do. Certainly the most creative people are intrinsically motivated in their work (Amabile 1983). Less creative people often pick a career for the money or prestige and are bored or loathe their career. These people don't do work that makes a difference in their field.

Helping students find what they really love to do is often hard and frustrating work. Yet, sharing the frustration with them now is better than leaving them to face it alone. To help students uncover their true interests, ask them to demonstrate a special talent or ability for the class. Explain that it doesn't matter what they do, only that they love the activity.

Watch as your students become animated as they discuss their presentations. Students who are not academically gifted are often thrilled to have their talents recognized and the presentations are usually fascinating, diverse, and enthusiastic. Whether it's floor exercises, a mini-fashion show, a hand-crafted lawn mower, a slide show of a garden, or an original song, you'll discover surprising things about your students that you can help them use in their assignments. For example, the boy who built a lawn mower gave his colonial America report on farm machinery.

Despite the possibility of finding some of your students' interest areas dull or distasteful, classroom demonstrations earn each child a niche with both teachers and peers, engender self-confidence (particularly for a student who does not excel in standard presentations), and capitalize on the student's enthusiasm. As students develop special talents and interests, they enjoy the accomplishments and feelings of self-worth.

Seeking Stimulating Environments

Help your students develop the ability to choose environments that stimulate their creativity. Although you try to present a stimulating classroom environment every day, your students spend many hours outside of school, eventually graduate, and either stagnate or grow in their creative development. Adults who continue to grow creatively visit and immerse themselves in environments that foster creativity.

To encourage students to develop skills in selecting environments that enhance creativity, choose some environments for the class to explore and help your students connect the environments with the experiences, creative growth, and accomplishment. Show students that creativity is easier with environmental stimulation.

Plan a field trip to a nearby museum, historical building, town hall, or other location with interesting displays and ask your students to generate and examine creative ideas for reports. Read excerpts from a book about a creative pioneer in the discipline being studied and the field-trip destination you've targeted—a great paleontologist if the focus is dinosaurs, or a great astronaut if the focus is space travel. Get students involved in role-playing (they can pretend to be newspaper reporters interviewing the great person), and have them make a list of interview questions.

Now take the class on the field-trip and encourage their creative insights, questions, discussions, and share your enjoyment of the environment. If you appear excited, your behavior will excite the students. When you return to school, ask the students about their new ideas— what are their report ideas? What characters would they role-play and how? What new ideas do they have? Make the connection between the environment and experience with their new level of creativity to show them that environments can stimulate creativity and the production of better products.

Once the students have written their reports, ask them how different the reports would have been had they not visited the destination. Again, make the connection explicit between a creativity-enhancing environment and later creative performance. Talk frequently about the motivation you get from these environments and challenge your students to explore other environments.

Your goal is to encourage your students to seek stimulating environments, to think about creative pursuits, and to energize them to do creative work. Teach them that activity is better than passivity and that mind-enriching activity facilitates significant accomplishments. Reward students for immersing themselves in stimulating environments—even the peace and quiet of their own bedrooms as they listen to music and plan compositions. Stress that, at its best, immersing oneself in stimulating environments is an active experience in which the mind is wholly engaged.

You can't reach into every nook of students' lives nor can you directly control their creative development in the years to come. But give them a lifelong gift by teaching them how to choose creative environments that help ideas flow. Knowing how to choose a creative environment is one of the best long-term strategies for developing creativity.

Playing to Strengths

Show students how to play to their strengths. By this point in our list of strategies, you've read quite a bit about getting students thinking about creative performance and encouraging them during the act of creating. Of course, as a teacher in a particular subject, you need to ensure that your subject matter is somehow involved. But as students grow in their creative insights and abilities, prepare them for creating in the world at large. In that arena they gain most by playing to their strengths.

Describe your strengths to your students and ask them to declare their strengths. As a group, brainstorm about how best to capitalize on these strengths. Let your students know that they facilitate creative performance by merging talent and preparation with opportunity. By helping students identify the exact nature of their talents, you create opportunities for them to express and use their talents.

We worked with one teacher who had two particularly difficult and unproductive students. He was so frustrated with the situation that he considered asking to have these students moved into another class. One student, Jed, never wanted to do any classwork or homework if it involved the printed word. The other student, Alicia, was incapacitated by the thought of failure. We encouraged the teacher to work with these two children and to teach them how to play to their strengths.

Jed remarked that one of his strengths was manual dexterity—he loved building model cars, assembling radios, and fixing small appliances. The fact that he was mechanically adept had not surfaced in the course of classroom interaction. After learning about Jed's strength, the teacher suggested that his next class project focus on motors and how they work—complete with a demonstration. Jed was excited by this idea and became enthusiastic and motivated: Instead of the typical class project, based on a book he would have found boring, he was able to do something he enjoyed. His project did include reading a book, but it was about how motors worked. Two weeks later, Jed's project culminated as a small working motor he had designed and built from scavenged and inexpensive parts.

Alicia was so sensitive, self-demanding, and intensely self-critical that a *90* on a spelling test upset her. Alicia was unable or unwilling to admit her strengths, so her teacher talked with her friends and learned about her love of dogs and her artistic abilities. As a result, the teacher suggested that Alicia borrow the school's camera to make a home movie about dogs—their evolution, biological properties, living habits, and modern uses. Alicia made a movie showing her dogs' teeth, eyes, ears, coats, and body shapes as she discussed the adaptation of mammals to a carnivorous lifestyle and modern breeding practices. Her film was amateurish yet creative and informative and the whole project played to Alicia's strengths and improved her self-esteem.

Any teacher can help students play to their strengths. All you need is flexibility in assignments and a willingness to help reluctant students determine the nature of their interests and strengths.

8 Viewing the Long-Term Perspective

Human salvation lies in the hands of the creatively maladjusted.

—Martin Luther King Jr.

Growing Creatively

Once we have a major creative idea, it's easy to spend the rest of our career following up on it. It's frightening to contemplate that the next idea may not be as good as the last one, or that success may disappear with the next idea. The result is that we can become complacent and stop being creative.

Sometimes, as experts, we become complacent and stop growing. We once heard a famous cognitive psychologist preface his talk with the remark that he had funded his own research because no one else would agree to fund him. Why? Because the work was in an area other than the one in which he had established a reputation. The funding agencies were willing to fund him in his usual area of expertise, but not in a new one. Later he became famous for work in the new area and easily obtained funding.

Teachers and administrators are susceptible to becoming victims of our own expertise—to become entrenched in ways of thinking that worked in the past, but not necessarily in the future (Frensch and Sternberg 1989). Being creative means stepping outside the boxes that we—and others—have created for ourselves.

Proselytizing for Creativity

Once you've mastered a few of these techniques to develop creativity and made them part of your daily teaching routine, spread the word. The virtues of teaching to develop creativity in students and ourselves multiply from reinforcement. Make the difference by telling your colleagues, associates, administrators, principal, school board members, and everyone else how important it is to develop creativity in students.

Use examples of creative student work, particularly from students who are not gifted in traditional academic abilities, to demonstrate the difference it makes to teach for creativity. Describe how every student can be reached with patience and a few techniques for developing creativity. Tell your colleagues that student projects are more interesting once students have experienced explicit creativity training. Richer, funnier, wilder, and generally far more interesting assignments, book reports, and projects make our lives less boring. It is, in fact, a good example of enlightened self-interest for teachers to give students creativity training, because creative students are more motivated and more involved with their schoolwork, and their work becomes more interesting.

ॐ   ॐ   ॐ

Closing Note

If you spread the word about the importance of teaching for creativity in schools, homes, and communities, this approach to teaching will become more common and benefit teachers and students everywhere. Small changes in the way questions are asked, assignments are worded, and tests are crafted can make big differences in the lives of students. We hope that we've provided ideas you can use immediately to start teaching for creativity.

References

Amabile, T.M. (1983). *The Social Psychology of Creativity*. New York: Springer-Verlag.

Arlin, P.K. (1990). "Wisdom: The Art of Problem Finding." In *Wisdom: Its Nature, Origins, and Development*, edited by R.J. Sternberg. New York: Cambridge University Press.

Boden, M. (1992). *The Creative Mind: Myths and Mechanisms*. New York: BasicBooks.

Brown, A.L., J.D. Bransford, R.A. Ferrara, and J.C. Campione (1983). "Learning, Remembering, and Understanding." Paul H. Mussen, ed. In *Handbook of Child Psychology: Cognitive Development*, Vol. 3, edited by J.H. Flavell and E.M. Markman. New York: Wiley.

Chen, Z., and M.W. Daehler. (1989). "Positive and Negative Transfer in Analogical Problem Solving by 6-Year-Old Children." *Cognitive Development* 4, 4: 327–344.

Chen, Z., and M.W. Daehler. (1992). "Intention and Outcome: Key Components of Causal Structure Facilitating Mapping in Children's Analogical Transfer." *Journal of Experimental Psychology* 53, 3: 237–257.

Clifford, M.M. (1988). "Failure Tolerance and Academic Risk Taking in Ten- to Twelve-Year Old Students." *British Journal of Educational Psychology* 58, 4: 15–27.

Csikszentmihalyi, M. (1988). "Society, Culture, and Person: A Systems View of Creativity." In *The Nature of Creativity*, edited by R.J. Sternberg. New York: Cambridge University Press.

Davidson, J.E., and R.J. Sternberg. (1984). "The Role of Insight in Intellectual Giftedness." *Gifted Child Quarterly* 28, 2: 58–64.

Dewey, J. (1933). *How We Think: A Restatement of the Relation of Reflective Thinking to the Educative Process*. Boston: D.C. Heath and Co.

Druckman, D., and R.A. Bjork, eds. (1991). *In the Mind's Eye: Enhancing Human Performance*. Washington, D.C.: National Academy Press.

Ericsson, K.A., R.T. Krampe, and C. Tesch-Römer. (1993). "The Role of Deliberate Practice in the Acquisition of Expert Performance." *Psychological Review* 100, 3: 363–406.

Fivush, R., J. Hudson, and K. Nelson. (1984). "Children's Long-Term Memory for a Novel Event: An Exploratory Study." *Merrill-Palmer Quarterly* 30, 3: 303–316.

Frensch, P.A., and R.J. Sternberg. (1989). "Expertise and Intelligent Thinking: When Is It Worse to Know Better?" In *Advances in the Psychology of Human Intelligence*, edited by R.J. Sternberg. Vol. 5. Hillsdale, N.J.: Lawrence Erlbaum.

Garcia, J., and R.A. Koelling. (1966). "The Relation of Cue to Consequence in Avoidance Learning." *Psychonomic Science* 4, 3: 123–124.

Gardner, H. (1993). *Creating Minds.* New York: BasicBooks.

Getzels, J.W., and M. Csikszentmihalyi. (1976). *The Creative Vision: A Longitudinal Study of Problem Finding in Art.* Chicago: Van Nostrand.

Ghiselin, B., ed. (1985). *The Creative Process: A Symposium.* Berkeley, Calif.: University of California Press. (Originally published in 1952.)

Gick, M.L., and K.J. Holyoak. (1980). "Analogical Problem Solving." *Cognitive Psychology,* 12, 3: 306–355.

Gick, M.L., and K.J. Holyoak. (1983). "Schema Induction and Analogical Transfer." *Cognitive Psychology,* 15, 1: 1–38.

Gruber, H.E. (1981). *Darwin on Man: A Psychological Study of Scientific Creativity.* 2nd ed. Chicago: University of Chicago Press. (Original work published in 1974 by Wildwood House, London.)

Gruber, H.E. (1986). "The Self-Construction of the Extraordinary." In *Conceptions of Giftedness,* edited by R.J. Sternberg and J.E. Davidson. New York: Cambridge University Press.

Hall, J.A. (1984). *Nonverbal Sex Differences: Accuracy of Communication and Expressive Style.* Baltimore: Johns Hopkins University Press.

Hammond, K.J. (1990). "Case-Based Planning: A Framework for Planning from Experience." *Cognitive Science* 14, 3: 385–443.

Hudson, J.A., and R. Fivush. (1991). "As Time Goes By: Sixth Graders Remember a Kindergarten Experience." *Applied Cognitive Psychology* 5, 4: 347–360.

John-Steiner, V. (1987). *Notebooks of the Mind: Explorations of Thinking.* New York: Perennial Library.

Mischel, W., Y. Shoda, and M.L. Rodriguez. (1989). "Delay of Gratification in Children." *Science* 244, 4907: 933–937.

Reed, S.K. (1989). "Constraints on the Abstraction of Solutions." *Journal of Educational Psychology* 81, 4: 532–540.

Resnick, L.B., J.M. Levine, and S.D. Teasley, eds. (1991). *Perspectives on Socially Shared Cognition.* Washington, D.C.: American Psychological Association.

Riesbeck, C.K., and R.C. Schank. (1989). *Inside Case-Based Reasoning.* Hillsdale, N.J.: L. Erlbaum.

Rosenthal, R., and L. Jacobson. (1968). *Pygmalion in the Classroom: Teacher Expectation and Pupils' Intellectual Development.* New York: Holt, Rinehart and Winston.

Rotter, J.B. (1966). *Generalized Expectancies for Internal Versus External Control of Reinforcement.* (Psychological Monographs No. 80; Whole No. 609). Washington, D.C.: American Psychological Association.

Rubenson, D.L., and M.A. Runco. (1992). "The Psychoeconomic Approach to Creativity." *New Ideas in Psychology* 10, 2: 131–147.

Schank, R.C. (1988). *The Creative Attitude: Learning to Ask and Answer the Right Questions.* New York: Macmillan.

Schrage, M. (1990). *Shared Minds: The New Technologies of Collaboration.* New York: Random House.

Simonton, D. (1988). *Scientific Genius: A Psychology of Science.* New York: Cambridge University Press.

Smith, E.E., and D.L. Medin. (1981). *Categories and Concepts.* Cambridge, Mass.: Harvard University Press.

Sternberg, R.J. (1985). *Beyond IQ: A Triarchic Theory of Human Intelligence.* New York: Cambridge University Press.

Sternberg, R.J. (1986). *Intelligence Applied.* Orlando, Fla: Harcourt Brace.

Sternberg, R.J. (1987). "Teaching Intelligence: The Application of Cognitive Psychology to the Improvement of Intellectual Skills." In *Teaching Thinking Skills: Theory and Practice*, edited by J.B. Baron and R.J. Sternberg. New York: Freeman.

Sternberg, R.J., ed. (1988a). *The Nature of Creativity: Contemporary Psychological Perspectives.* New York: Cambridge University Press.

Sternberg, R.J. (1988b). *The Triarchic Mind: A New Theory of Human Intelligence.* New York: Viking.

Sternberg, R.J. (1994). "Answering Questions and Questioning Answers: Guiding Children to Intellectual Excellence." *Phi Delta Kappan* 76, 2: 136–138.

Sternberg, R.J., and T.I. Lubart. (1991). "An Investment Theory of Creativity and Its Development." *Human Development* 34, 1: 1–31.

Sternberg, R.J., and T.I. Lubart. (1995). *Defying the Crowd: Cultivating Creativity in a Culture of Conformity.* New York: Free Press.

Stevenson, H.W., and J.W. Stigler. (1992). *The Learning Gap.* New York: Summit.

Thorkildsen, T.A. (1989). "Justice in the Classroom: The Student's View." *Child Development* 60, 2: 323–334.

Thorkildsen, T.A. (1991). "Defining Social Goods and Distributing Them Fairly: The Development of Conceptions of Fair Testing Practices." *Child Development* 62, 6: 852–863.

Vygotsky, L. (1978). *Mind in Society.* Cambridge, Mass.: Harvard University Press.

Wagenaar, W.A. (1986). "My Memory: A Study of Autobiographical Memory over Six Years." *Cognitive Psychology* 18, 2: 225–252.

Williams, W.M., T. Blythe, N. White, R.J. Sternberg, J. Li, and H.I. Gardner. (1996). *Practical Intelligence for School: A Handbook for Teachers of Grades 5–8.* New York: HarperCollins.